GEORGIA LAW REQUIRES LIBRARY
MATERIALS TO BE RETURNED OR
REPLACEMENT COSTS PAID.
(O.C.G.A. 20-5-53)

No Lex 12-12

PEACHTREE CITY
PLAN TO STAY™

Miley Cyrus

Amie Jane Leavitt

P.O. Box 196
Hockessin, Delaware 19707
Visit us on the web: www.mitchelllane.com
Comments? email us: mitchelllane@mitchelllane.com

Mitchell Lane PUBLISHERS

Printing   7   8   9

A Robbie Reader
Contemporary Biography

Albert Pujols	Alex Rodriguez	Aly and AJ
Amanda Bynes	Ashley Tisdale	Brittany Murphy
Charles Schulz	Dakota Fanning	Dale Earnhardt Jr.
Donovan McNabb	Drake Bell & Josh Peck	Dr. Seuss
Dwayne "The Rock" Johnson	Dylan & Cole Sprouse	Eli Manning
Hilary Duff	Jamie Lynn Spears	Jessie McCartney
Johnny Gruelle	Jonas Brothers	Jordin Sparks
LeBron James	Mia Hamm	**Miley Cyrus**
Miranda Cosgrove	Raven Symone	Shaquille O'Neal
The Story of Harley-Davidson	Syd Hoff	Tiki Barber
Tom Brady	Tony Hawk	

Library of Congress Cataloging-in-Publication Data
Leavitt, Amie Jane.
    Miley Cyrus / by Amie Jane Leavitt.
        p. cm. — (A Robbie reader)
    Includes bibliographical references (p.   ) and index.
    ISBN-13: 978-1-58415-590-4 (library bound)
    1. Cyrus, Miley, 1992—Juvenile literature. 2. Singers—United States—Biography—Juvenile literature. 3. Actresses—United States—Biography—Juvenile literature.
I. Title.
ML3930.C98L43 2008
782.42164092—dc22   2007000812

ABOUT THE AUTHOR: Amie Jane Leavitt is an accomplished author and photographer. She graduated from Brigham Young University as an education major and has since then taught all subjects and grade levels in both private and public schools. She has written dozens of books for kids, has contributed to online and print media, and has worked as a consultant, writer, and editor for numerous educational publishing and assessment companies. Amie enjoys writing about young people who are working hard to achieve their dreams.

PHOTO CREDITS: Cover, pp. 8, 10—David Longendyke/ Globe Photos; pp. 4, 11, 22—Nina Prommer/ Globe Photos; p. 6—Tim Mosenfelder/ Getty Images; p. 7—Stephen Shugerman/ Getty Images; p. 12—Michael Germana/ Globe Photos; p. 14—Brian Ach/ Wire Image; pp. 16, 24—Barry Talesnick/ Globe Photos; pp. 18, 25—Michael Buckner/ Getty Images; p. 19—Kevin Winter/ Getty Images; p. 21—John Barrett/Globe Photos.

ACKNOWLEDGMENTS: The following story has been thoroughly researched, and to the best of our knowledge represents a true story. While every possible effort has been made to ensure accuracy, the publisher will not assume liability for damages caused by inaccuracies in the data, and makes no warranty on the accuracy of the information contained herein. This story has not been authorized or endorsed by Miley Cyrus.

PLB / PLB2 / PLB2 / PLB2,28 / PLB2,27,28 / PLB2,28

TABLE OF CONTENTS

Chapter One
Big Break 5

Chapter Two
Smiley Miley 9

Chapter Three
Young Lucille Ball 13

Chapter Four
Hannah Montana 17

Chapter Five
Best Friends 23

Chronology 27
Filmography 28
Discography 28
Find Out More 29
Works Consulted 29
Glossary 31
Index 32

A shout-out to her fans. Miley arrives at the Shrine Auditorium in Los Angeles for the American Music Awards in November 2006.

Big Break

Miley Cyrus was only eleven when she first tried out for the part of Hannah Montana. The people at Disney thought she was too young and small for the part. Even so, they must have liked what they saw. They kept asking her to come back for more **auditions** (aw-DIH-shuns) over the next two years. Miley grew up during that time. Maybe now she would be what they were looking for.

On the day of Miley's final audition, she walked into a room full of important Disney businesspeople. This time, her performance really impressed them. "She stood in front of us and knocked us out," said Disney Channel Entertainment president, Gary Marsh.

Finally, the people at Disney made their decision. Miley Cyrus got a phone call. She had been chosen. One thousand girls had tried out for the part. Out of all of them, they had chosen her!

Miley had spent years working toward this goal. She had taken acting lessons. She had tried out for many parts. Then, she finally got her biggest break yet. She was going to play the two roles of Miley Stewart and Hannah

Miley sings a hit from *Hannah Montana* at the HP Pavilion in San Jose, California, in September 2006. She loves performing.

Miley poses for the photographers with her dad, Billy Ray Cyrus. He is a famous country singer who also plays in *Hannah Montana* with Miley.

Montana on the new Disney Channel TV show *Hannah Montana.*

After Miley got her part, she got another surprise. Her dad would have a part on the show too. He was going to play the part of her father. He was nervous at first. He didn't want to mess up his daughter's show. In the end, he decided to take the part. Miley was excited to be working with her dad on her first television show.

Smiling pretty for the camera. Miley is known for her cute smile and bubbly personality.

Smiley Miley

Miley Cyrus was born on November 23, 1992, in Franklin, Tennessee. Her dad is Billy Ray Cyrus. He is a famous country singer. He sings many popular songs, including "Achy Breaky Heart." He is also an actor. He starred on the PAX TV show *Doc*. Miley's mom is Leticia (leh-TIH-shuh) Finley Cyrus. People call her Tish. Tish helps Miley as her manager.

The name on Miley's birth certificate is Destiny Hope Cyrus. Her parents chose this name because they had *hope* that she would have a great future, or *destiny*. They have definitely been right so far. Why do people call her Miley? As a baby, she was very happy and smiled all the time. Her dad would always call her Smiley or Miley. The nickname stuck. She's been Miley ever since. Even now, she is still a very happy person. Her cute smile is one of the first things people notice about her.

Miley has five brothers and sisters. Their names are Brandi, Trace, Christopher Cody, Braison Chance, and Noah. Miley grew up on a 500-acre farm in Thompson's Station, Tennessee. This town is near Nashville. Miley loves the country, especially her animals. She

Two of a kind. People say that Miley is just like her mother, Tish. Tish also works as Miley's manager.

Miley and her dad just finished zipping along the tracks of a roller coaster on Santa Monica Pier. It's National Boys and Girls Club Day there, and the Cyrus stars are hosting a party.

has many pets. She has dogs, cats, horses, cows, and even chickens. Probably her favorite pet is her dog, Loco.

Just like other kids, Miley has many hobbies. She likes to dance, sing, cheerlead, play the guitar, and write music. She also loves to go shopping with her mom, especially when she's buying shoes. Miley likes wearing many different styles. She can go from being punky one day to preppy the next.

11

Miley considers her dad to be a good friend. They enjoy working together every day on the set of *Hannah Montana*.

Young Lucille Ball

Miley has always been an entertainer at heart. She told a magazine reporter in 2007, "When I was little, I would stand up on couches and say, 'Watch me.' I've always loved singing, and I've always loved acting and dancing.' "

When Billy Ray toured as a country music entertainer, Miley would sometimes perform on stage with him. Her parents knew then that their little daughter was a star. "She's the real deal musically," Billy Ray says. "Since she was little, she would look at me confidently and say, 'I'm going to blow by you, Daddy. I'm going to be a singer, songwriter, entertainer.'"

Billy Ray also says that Miley has a funny personality. He calls her a young Lucille (loo-

13

On stage with a microphone in her hand, Miley feels right at home. In October 2006, she performed music from a Walt Disney album on MTV's Total Request Live.

SEEL) Ball. Lucille Ball was a famous **comedian** (kuh-MEE-dee-un) from the 1950s. She had her own TV show called *I Love Lucy*. Lucille Ball always did crazy things on her show. It is a **compliment** (KAHM-pleh-ment) to be compared to this famous **actress** (AK-tres).

Although Miley has a famous father, she has worked hard to get her own parts in movies and on TV. She didn't want people to know her as Billy Ray's daughter. She wanted to get the parts because she was **talented** (TAA-len-ted).

Miley started trying out for parts when she was very young. She practiced a lot and tried hard at the auditions. Many times she would not get the part even if she did her best. Yet Miley never gave up. She just tried to be better the next time.

Miley's first big break came in 2003. She got the part of Ruthie on the movie *Big Fish*. Then, she got to play some parts on her dad's show, *Doc*. It was after playing these parts that Miley realized how much she liked acting. Her dad said she should just be a kid and have fun. He thought acting would make her grow up too fast. But Miley had already made up her mind. She wanted to be an actress.

"Shhh, it's a secret." Miley copies her famous pose from the cover of her *Hannah Montana* album. In two months the album sold 1.6 million copies.

Hannah Montana

Miley loves starring in *Hannah Montana.* The show is about a young girl named Miley Stewart. This character moves to Los Angeles from Tennessee with her brother and father. Miley Stewart has a secret **identity** (eye-DEN-tih-tee). She is a famous teen rock star named Hannah Montana. During the day she is a normal kid at school. At night, she dresses up in fancy clothes and sings onstage. Miley Stewart doesn't want anyone to know about her secret. She is afraid the kids at school will treat her differently. Only her family and her two best friends know that she is Hannah Montana.

Miley Cyrus has a few things in common with both Miley Stewart and Hannah Montana. On the show, Miley Stewart goes through the same stuff that all young girls go through. She has a crush on a boy and doesn't know how to act around him. She has fights with her friends sometimes. She doesn't always get along with her brother.

Jason Earles plays Miley's brother on *Hannah Montana*. He says that Miley is "an adorable, energetic fourteen-year-old girl. . . . She's about as sweet a person as you could want."

Don't these three Disney stars look like they could be sisters? Well, two of them are! Here, Miley (left) poses with her pals Aly and AJ Michalka.

Miley also thinks it is fun playing the part of Hannah. She gets to wear a blond wig for this part. The wig is itchy and hot, but Miley enjoys looking different. She also gets to wear a lot of makeup, wear dark sunglasses, and dress up in rock-star clothes. Most girls only dream about getting to dress up and perform onstage. Miley is lucky to do it every day!

Dressed up like Hannah Montana with her sparkly clothes and shiny blond wig, Miley performs onstage for her fans.

Miley was in the Macy's Thanksgiving Day Parade in New York City. This is a huge honor for any star. Afterward, she hung out in the rain signing autographs for her fans.

Some of the songs Miley sings on the show are "This Is the Life," "Best of Both Worlds," and "The Other Side of Me." She is such a good singer that Hollywood Records has asked her to record four albums for them. This is good news for all the fans who like to hear Miley sing.

In September 2006, Miley and her dad hosted the National Boys and Girls Club Day at Santa Monica Pier in California. After a day riding amusement park rides and playing on the beach, Miley performed a few numbers for her fans.

Best Friends

Miley was sad to leave her friends in Tennessee when she moved to Los Angeles in December 2005. But it wasn't too long before she made some new friends in Hollywood.

Many people hope that the characters on a TV show are also friends in real life. Sometimes this happens and sometimes it doesn't. In Miley's case, it has. She is very good friends with Emily Osment and Mitchel Musso (MOO-soh), her costars on *Hannah Montana*. Emily plays Miley's best friend, Lilly. Mitchel plays her guy-friend, Oliver. The three enjoy working with one another. They also like hanging out together off the set. They

Out on the town. Miley and her father tour the Big Apple in January 2007.

Mitchel Musso, right, plays Oliver, one of Hannah Montana's best friends on the show. The two have fun clowning around on the set as well as off.

spend hours talking on the phone at night. During the daytime, they send text messages on their cell phones between scenes.

Miley is also very good friends with her dad. She says they have so much in common that they are almost like the same person. She likes it when she gets to do silly things to him on the show. Sometimes she gets to drop food on him. Sometimes she gets to hit him in the face with a cake. These are definitely things she couldn't do in real life. That's what makes working on the show so much fun.

Miley signs a guitar for a charity auction held in Hollywood. She believes in helping others whenever she can.

Miley credits her faith for her success. She says, "That's kind of why I'm like here in Hollywood—to be like a light, a testimony to say God can take someone from Nashville and make me this, but it's his will that made this happen."

Miley hopes to continue acting and singing for the rest of her life. Hopefully, for all her fans, she'll get her wish!

1992   Miley Cyrus is born in Franklin, Tennessee, on November 23.

1994   Her brother Braison Chance is born on May 9.

2000   Her sister Noah Lindsey is born on January 8.

2003   Miley plays the role of Ruthie in *Big Fish*. She plays the role of Kylie on PAX TV's *Doc*. She starts trying out for *Hannah Montana*.

2004   Miley receives a Daisy Rock guitar (a guitar line made especially for girls) from her parents in front of 30,000 of her father's fans on June 13, and she becomes tween spokesperson for Daisy Rock.

2005   The first episode of *Hannah Montana* is taped on December 16.

2006   The first episode of *Hannah Montana* airs on Disney Channel on March 24 and is viewed by 5.4 million people. Miley signs a four-album record deal with Hollywood Records. The sound track from *Hannah Montana* comes out on October 24 and is number 1 on the Billboard Top 200 Chart. Within two months, it sells over 1.6 million copies.

2007   Miley performs at RodeoHouston before a sold-out crowd of over 73,000 people; *Hannah Montana* is the number one show in its time slot for kids ages six to fourteen. *Hannah Montana 2: Meet Miley Cyrus* debuts at Number 1 on the Billboard Top 200 Chart. Miley wins two Teen Choice Awards: Choice Summer Artist and Best TV Actress in a Comedy Series. Her Best of Both Worlds Tour is a huge hit.

2008   The 3-D movie *Hannah Montana and Miley Cyrus: Best of Both Worlds Concert Tour* is released in theaters, and *Hannah Montana: One in a Million* is released on video. Miley's song "See You Again" is a Top-20 hit. Miley is honored to be a presenter at the Academy Awards. She begins shooting a third Hannah Montana movie.

Filmography

2008	*Hannah Montana/Miley Cyrus: Best of Both Worlds Concert Tour*
	Hannah Montana: One in a Million (Video)
2006–2008	*Hannah Montana* (TV series)
2006	*The Suite Life of Zack and Cody* (TV series)
2003	*Big Fish*
	Doc (TV series)

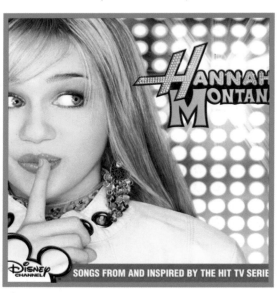

Discography

2008	*Breakout*
2007	*Hannah Montana 2: Meet Miley Cyrus*
2006	*Hannah Montana*

Articles

Bryson, Jodi. "The Secret Life of Miley Cyrus."
    Girls' Life. December/January 2007.
Doveala, Emily. "Who Is Hannah Montana?"
    Time for Kids. April 18, 2006.

Works Consulted

Beck, Ken. "Teen Miley Cyrus Leaves
    Tennessee Hills for Hollywood—With
    Dad Billy Ray in Tow." *Tennessean.com.*
    March 19, 2006.
Beck, Marilyn, and Stacy Jenel Smith. "Like
    Father." *U-Entertainment.* April 26, 2006.
Bianculli, David. " 'Montana' Is State of the Art."
    New York Daily News. March 23, 2006.
Clark, Champ. "Her Big Breaky." *People.*
    April 17, 2006, p. 117.
Guthrie, Marisa. "Making Dad's Achy, Breaky
    Heart Swell with Pride." *New York Daily
    News.* September 13, 2005.
Learmonth, Michael. "Disney Wishes on New
    Tween Star." *Variety.* February 20, 2006,
    pp. 18–19.

Levin, Gary. "Disney Finds Place for Tweens." *USA Today*. October 27, 2005.

Luck Media & Marketing, Inc: *Daisy Rock Girl Guitars,* "Billy Ray Cyrus and Wife Tish Surprise Daughter Miley with Daisy Rock Girl Guitar at Fan Club Event During CMA Music Festival." http://www.luckmedia.com/daisyrock/photogallery.html

Oldenburg, Ann. "Lifelong Work Pays Off, Says Miley Cyrus, 13." *USA Today*. March 24, 2006.

Smith, Ethan. "The Big Golden Beat of Little Hannah Montana." *The Wall Street Journal*. January 2, 2007. http://content.hamptonroads.com/story.cfm?story=116871&ran=70694

Steinberg, Jacques. "Hannah Montana and Miley Cyrus: A Tale of Two Tweens." *The New York Times*. April 20, 2006.

Walstad, David. "There's No Achy Heart for Billy Ray." *MySA.com*. March 23, 2006.

actress (AK-tres)—a woman who performs in a play, television show, or movie.

auditions (aw-DIH-shuns)—tryouts for a part in a play, television show, or movie.

comedian (kuh-MEE-dee-un)—a person whose job it is to tell jokes and make people laugh.

compliment (KAHM-pleh-ment)—a nice thing to say to someone.

identity (eye-DEN-tih-tee)—who a person is.

talented (TAA-lin-ted)—having certain skills or abilities.

"Achy Breaky Heart" 9

American Music Awards 4

Ball, Lucille 13–14

Big Fish 15

Cyrus, Billy Ray (father) 7, 9, 11, 12, 13, 15, 22, 24

Cyrus, Miley (Destiny Hope)
  birth of 9
  brothers, sisters of 10
  and charity events 11, 22, 26
  childhood of 11, 13, 15
  hobbies of 11, 25
  music of 6, 13, 14, 20, 21, 22, 26
  nickname of 9–10
  personality of 8, 9–10, 13–14, 18
  pets of 11

Cyrus, Tish (Leticia Finley, mother) 9–10

Disney Channel 5–6, 7, 19

Doc 9, 15

Earles, Jason 18

Hannah Montana 5–7, 12, 16, 17–19, 20, 21, 23, 25, 26

Hollywood 18, 23, 26

Hollywood Records 21

Loco (dog) 11

Los Angeles, California 4, 17, 23

Macy's Thanksgiving Day Parade 21

Marsh, Gary 5

Michalka, Aly and AJ 19

MTV 14

Musso, Mitchel 23, 25

Osment, Emily 23, 25

Pax TV 9

Tennessee 9–10, 17, 23